WORD PROBLEMS
USING
ADDITION
AND
SUBTRACTION

MASTERING MATH WORD PROBLEMS

Zella Williams and
Rebecca Wingard-Nelson

Enslow Publishing
101 W. 23rd Street
Suite 240
New York, NY 10011
USA

enslow.com

Published in 2017 by Enslow Publishing, LLC.
101 W. 23rd Street, Suite 240, New York, NY 10011

Library of Congress Cataloging-in-Publication Data

Names: Williams, Zella, author. | Wingard-Nelson, Rebecca, author.
Title: Word problems using addition and subtraction / Zella Williams and Rebecca Wingard-Nelson.
Description: New York, NY : Enslow Publishing, 2017. | Series: Mastering math word problems | Includes bibliographical references and index.
Identifiers: LCCN 2016021415| ISBN 9780766082540 (library bound) | ISBN 9780766082526 (pbk.) | ISBN 9780766082533 (6-pack)
Subjects: LCSH: Word problems (Mathematics)—Juvenile literature. | Problem solving—Juvenile literature. | Addition—Juvenile literature. | Subtraction—Juvenile literature.
Classification: LCC QA63 .W564 2017 | DDC 513.2—dc23
LC record available at https://lccn.loc.gov/2016021415

Printed in China

To Our Readers: We have done our best to make sure all websites in this book were active and appropriate when we went to press. However, the author and the publisher have no control over and assume no liability for the material available on those websites or on any websites they may link to. Any comments or suggestions can be sent by e-mail to customerservice@enslow.com.

Portions of this book originally appeared in the book *Animal Word Problems Starring Addition and Subtraction*.

Photo Credits: Cover, p. 1 © iStockphoto.com/dagmar heymans; pp. 3, 32 tonyz20/Shutterstock.com; p. 4 Comstock Images/Stockbyte/Thinkstock; p. 5 (book) Maximilian Laschon/Shutterstock.com; p. 7 (top) skynesher/E+/Getty Images; p. 7 (bottom) Encyclopaedia Britannica/Universal Images Group/Getty Images; p. 10 Jonathan Kirn/Photographer's Choice/Getty Images; p. 11 wasantistock/iStock/Thinkstock; p. 13 Erik Tham/Corbis Documentary/Getty Images; p. 16 Mikhail Kolesnikov/Shutterstock.com; p. 18 Danita Delimont/Gallo Images/Getty Images; p. 20 ChGR/E+/Getty Images; p. 22 UIG Platinum/Universal Images Group/Getty Images; p. 24 Jiang Zhongyan/Shutterstock.com; p. 26 Spring Disney/Flickr Flash/Getty Images; p. 28 BoxerX/Shutterstock.com; p. 30 Wayne Morra/EyeEm/Getty Images; p. 34 Heiko Kiera/Shutterstock.com; p. 36 Mr. Suttipon Yakham/Shutterstock.com; p. 38 Animals Animals/SuperStock; p. 40 visceralimage/Shutterstock.com; p. 42 Steve West/Oxford Scientific/Getty Images; p. 44 Weldon Schloneger/Shutterstock.com; p. 47 bluelela/Shutterstock.com; cover and interior pages icons and graphics Shutterstock.com: Anna_leni (owl), Draze Design (pad and pencil), RedlineVector (light bulb), Yuri Gayvoronskiy (eyes), james Weston (scrambled numbers), Ratoca (thumbs up), BeRad (magnifying glass), Grimgram (pencil).

Contents

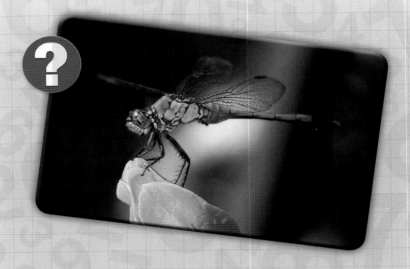

Tackling Word Problems

5

Identifying the Operation

13

What Information Do I Need?

20

When in Doubt, Draw!

24

Math with Zeros

26

Using Place-Value Drawings

30

Solving Problems with Mental Math

36

Multi-Digit Problems

40

It's OK to Estimate

44

Glossary

46

For More Information

47

Index

48

Learning new things can be hard. Stick with it and you'll soon be solving word problems like a pro!

Tackling Word Problems

 ## Tips to Keep in Mind

Word problems might show up in your homework, on a test, or in your life. These tips can help you solve them, no matter where they appear.

 ## Be positive!

When you get a problem right the <u>first</u> time, good for you! When you don't get a problem right the first time, but you learn from your mistakes, that is awesome! You learned something new!

 ## Get help early!

New problems build on old ones. If you don't understand today's problem, tomorrow's problem will be even harder to understand.

In some problems, you will see clue spotters. A magnifying glass will help you spy clue words in the problem.

 Do your homework!

The more you practice anything, the better you become at it. You can't play an instrument or play a sport well without practice. Homework problems are your practice.

Move on!

If you get stuck, move to the next problem. Do the ones you know how to solve first. You'll feel more confident. And you won't miss the ones you know because you ran out of time. Go back later and try the problems you skipped.

Ask questions!

When someone is helping you, asking good questions tells the person what you don't understand. If you don't ask questions, you will never get answers!

Take a break!

If you have tried everything you can think of but are only getting frustrated, take a break. Close your eyes and take a deep breath. Stretch your arms and legs. Get a drink of water or a snack. Then come back and try again.

Don't give up!

The first time you try to solve a word problem, you might come up with an answer that does not make sense or that you know is not right. Don't give up! Check your math. Try solving the problem a different way. If you quit, you won't learn.

Don't be afraid to raise your hand and ask for help.

! Take It Step by Step

Word problems may seem complicated. They can be solved by following four easy steps, though.

? Here's a problem:

One kind of stickleback fish has five spines on its back. Another kind of stickleback has three. If the fish swim together, how many spines are there in all?

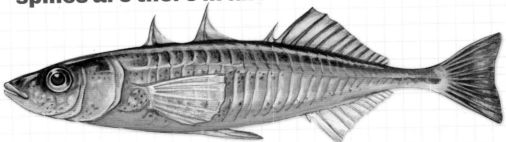

This is a drawing of a three-spined stickleback fish.

Now let's solve the problem using four steps.

 ## Step 1 Read and understand the problem.

Read the problem carefully.
Put the problem in your own words.

What do you know?
One stickleback has **five** spines.
One stickleback has **three** spines.

What are you trying to find?
The number of spines the fish have **together**.

 ## Step 2 Make a plan.

Some problems tell you what plan to use. They may tell you to make a table or draw a picture to solve the problem. For other problems, you make your own plan. Use whatever plan makes the most sense and is easiest for you. Some plans you might try are:

Look for a pattern	**Write an equation**
Draw a picture	**Use a model**
Estimate	**Break it apart**

How can you solve this problem?

You can write an equation. The clue word "**together**" tells you to add the number of spines on each fish.

Step 3 Solve the problem.

It is time to do the math!
If you find that your plan is not working, make a
new plan. Don't give up the first time.

Let's write an equation.
One stickleback has 5 spines, the other has 3 spines.
Add the number of spines.

5 + 3=8

If the two fish swim together, there are 8 spines in all.
Write your answer. Make sure you include the units.

Step 4 Look back.

The problem is solved! But you aren't finished yet.
Take a good look at your answer.

Does it make sense? Did you include the units?
Did you use the right numbers to begin?
Yes.

Is the math correct?
Yes, 5 + 3 = 8.

Is there another way to solve the problem?
Yes, you can draw a picture and count the spines.
Try the other plan and see if you get the same answer.
You can count 8 spines on the two fish. Either plan
gives the same answer, 8 spines. **You just solved a**
word problem!

Write a Number Sentence

Do you know what an equation is?

An equation is a sentence that uses numbers. Changing a word problem into a number sentence can help you solve it.

 ## Here's a problem.

An inchworm took 3 hours to crawl up a tree. It took 2 more hours to crawl along a branch to a leaf. In all, how long did it take the inchworm to reach the leaf? Write an equation to show how long it took.

Solving a problem two different ways is a great way to check your work.

Inchworms are the larva, or babies, of geometer moths.

Read and understand.

What do you know?

The inchworm took 3 hours to crawl up the tree.
It took 2 hours to crawl along the branch.

What are you trying to find?

How long it took the inchworm to reach the leaf.

Plan.

The problem tells us to find the answer, then write an equation to show what happened.
Let's find the answer by counting on.

Solve.

The inchworm took 3 hours to crawl up the tree.
Start at 3. It took 2 more hours to crawl along the branch.
Start at 3, then count two more: 4, 5.
It took the inchworm 5 hours in all to reach the leaf.

Now, write the equation.

Think about the whole story.

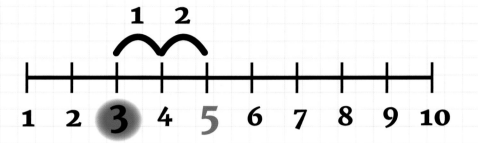

3 hours up tree + **2** hours along branch = **5** hours

3 + 2 = 5

 ## Look back.

Does the answer make sense?

Yes.

Did you answer the right question?

Yes.

Identifying the Operation

❗ Identifying Addition Problems

*Addition and subtraction are called operations.
How can you tell if a word problem is an
addition problem?
You need to look for clues.*

❓ Here's the problem.

Mia has geckos living in her garden. There
are 5 types of geckos that are active at night.
There are 2 other types of geckos that
are active during the day. How many
types of geckos are in Mia's garden in total?

This is a
species of
day gecko.
It is called
a green
Madagascar
day gecko.

Read and understand.

What do you know?

Mia has 5 types of night geckos in her garden.
She also has 2 types of day geckos.

What are you trying to find?

How many types of geckos are in Mia's garden.

Are there any clue words in the problem?

Clue words are words that tell you what kind of equation you can write to solve the problem. Here are some clue words that tell you when a problem uses addition: **add**, **combined**, **sum**, **total**, **plus**, **in all**, **together**, **increase**, **both**.

This problem uses the clue word "**total**."
It is an addition problem.

Mia has geckos living in her garden. There are 5 types of geckos that are active at night. There are 2 other types of geckos that are active during the day. How many types of geckos are in Mia's garden in total?

Problems that combine groups, such as night geckos and day geckos, are addition problems.

Plan.

Let's write an addition equation.

Solve.

Write an equation that uses the numbers from the problem.

$$
\begin{aligned}
&\ \ 5 \text{ types of night geckos} \\
+&\ \ 2 \text{ types of day geckos} \\
\hline
&\ \ 7 \text{ types of geckos total}
\end{aligned}
$$

Mia has 7 types of geckos in her garden.

Look back.

Does the answer make sense?
Yes.

Is the math correct?
Yes, 5 + 2 = 7.

Identifying Subtraction Problems

How can you tell if a word problem is a subtraction problem? There are clues here, too.

Here's the problem.

Two toucans tossed 8 red berries and 6 yellow berries back and forth to each other. How many more red berries did they toss than yellow berries?

Read and understand.

Toucans are best known for their large, often colorful, bills.

What do you know?

The toucans tossed 8 red berries.
The toucans tossed 6 yellow berries.

What are you trying to find?

How many more red berries were tossed than yellow berries.

Are there any clue words in the problem?

Here are some clue words that tell you when a problem uses subtraction: **subtract**, **difference**, **take away**, **how much less**, **how many more**, **remain**, **left**, **fewer**.

This problem uses the clue words "**how many more**." It is a subtraction problem.

Two toucans tossed 8 red berries and 6 yellow berries back and forth to each other. **How many more** red berries did they toss than yellow berries?

Problems that find the difference between two amounts are subtraction problems.

Plan.

Let's write a subtraction equation.

Solve.

To find the difference between two amounts, begin with the larger value and subtract the smaller value.
Begin with the number of red berries, 8.
Subtract the number of yellow berries, 6.

$8 - 6 = 2$

The toucans tossed 2 more red berries than they did yellow berries.

Look back.

Is the math correct?
Yes, $8 - 6 = 2$.

Opposites

Addition and subtraction are inverse operations.
They do the opposite of each other.
You can use inverse operations to check
your answers.

Here's the problem.

Manny has 9 tarantulas. When he woke
up, only 2 were in the cage. How many
tarantulas had escaped?

Read and understand.

Tarantulas are
a kind of large,
fuzzy spider.
Their bite can
be venomous.

What do you know?
Manny has 9 tarantulas.
2 were in the cage.

What are you trying to find?

The number of tarantulas that had escaped.

What kind of problem is this?

There were some tarantulas, then some went away. This is subtraction.

Plan.

Write a subtraction equation.

Solve.

```
   9 tarantulas
 − 2 tarantulas in cage
   ─────────────────
   7 tarantulas escaped
```

There were 7 tarantulas that escaped.

Look back.

You can check the answer to a subtraction problem by using addition.

Add the answer (7) to the number you subtracted (2). $7 + 2 = 9$

If the sum (9) is the number you started with, then your answer is correct.

Did you start with 9?

Yes.

What Information Do I Need?

❗ Is There Enough Information?

When you do not have enough information, you cannot solve a word problem.

❓ Here's the problem:

Ring-tailed lemurs are about 18 inches long. Their tails are longer than their bodies. There are 23 rings on their tails. How much longer is a lemur's tail than its body?

🦉 Read and understand.

The lemur's body is about 18 inches long.
Its tail is longer than its body.
Its tail has 23 rings.

You can really see how long a ring-tailed lemur's tail is from this picture!

Plan.

The clue words "**how much longer**" tell you this is a subtraction problem. Subtract the length of the lemur's body from the length of its tail.

Solve.

There is not enough information. The problem does not tell you how long the tail is.

Look back.

Read the problem again. Was the information given and you just missed it? No, the problem does not tell you how long the tail is.

Too Much Information!

Some problems give more information than you need. This can be confusing!

Here's the problem.

Some hens, like Rhode Island Reds and Orpingtons, lay brown eggs. Leghorn hens lay white eggs. The McMurray family has 6 Rhode Island Red hens, 4 Orpington hens, and 10 Leghorn hens. They also have 9 Araucana hens that lay blue eggs. How many hens do they have that lay brown eggs in all?

Read and understand.

What do you know?

Underline the types of hens in the problem so that you don't miss any. Sort what you know by making a chart of the hens, how many of each, and what color eggs they lay.

These are Rhode Island Red hens.
They lay brown eggs.

What are you trying to find?

The number of hens that lay brown eggs.

 Plan.

Let's add only the hens that lay brown eggs.

Type	Number	Egg color
Rhode Island Red	6	Brown
Orpington	4	Brown
Leghorn	10	White
Araucana	9	Blue

Solve.

  6 Rhode Island Red hens
+ 4 Orpington hens
 10 hens that lay brown eggs

The McMurrays have 10 hens that lay brown eggs.

Look back.

Did you use the right information?
Yes.

Does your answer match the problem?
Yes.

When in Doubt, Draw!

Does a word problem have you stumped? A picture can help you find the answer to a problem.

? Here's the problem.

**An orangutan picked 9 mangos.
It threw 3 of the mangos into the bushes.
How many were left?**

Read and understand.

Mangos grow in tropical, or warm, places. They are a good food source for many animals.

What do you know?

The orangutan picked 9 mangos.
It threw 3 away.

What are you trying to find?

The number of mangos that were left.

Plan.

Let's draw a picture to solve the problem.

Solve.

Your picture does not need to be perfect.

You can use circles to show the mangos.

Draw a picture to show the 9 mangos that were picked.

Cross off the 3 mangos that were thrown away.

Count the mangos that are left in the picture.

There are 6.

There are 6 what? There are 6 orangutans?

NO! There are 6 mangos.

Make sure you tell the whole answer.

There were 6 mangos left.

Look back.

Does the answer make sense?

Yes.

Have you seen problems like this before?

Yes, this problem had some things (mangos), then some went away.

What kind of problem is this?

It is a subtraction problem.

Math with Zeros

! Adding Zero

Some problems are easy to solve when you know about zeros.

? Here's the problem.

An opossum ate 27 grubs in the morning. It did not eat any grubs in the afternoon. How many grubs did it eat in all ?

Read and understand.

Opossums are omnivores. That means they will eat whatever is available!

What do you know?

The opossum ate 27 grubs in the morning. It ate zero more in the afternoon.

What are you trying to find?

The number of grubs the opossum ate in all.

Plan.

Since the opossum ate zero grubs in the afternoon, you can use what you know about zeros to answer the question.

Solve.

When you add or subtract a zero, the original number does not change.

The opossum ate 27 grubs in the morning and zero more in the afternoon. Zero is nothing, so in all the opossum ate only the 27 grubs from the morning. The opossum ate 27 grubs in all.

Look back.

Does the answer make sense?

Yes.

Did you include the units in the answer?

Yes.

The Answer Is . . . Zero!

When you take away everything, zero is always left.

Here's the problem.

Eight ducks were all quacking at a dog. The dog barked. Eight ducks ran away. How many ducks were left?

Ducks live on and near water. They swim in groups looking for food.

Read and understand.

What do you know?

There were 8 ducks. They were all quacking.
All 8 ducks ran away.

What are you trying to find?

The number of ducks left.
Is there anything special about this problem?
Yes, the numbers are the same. All 8 ducks ran away.

Plan.

Let's use what you know about zeros.

Solve.

When you take away the same number you start with, the answer is always zero.

We started with 8 ducks. All 8 of them ran away. There were none, or zero, left.

There are no ducks left.

Look back.

Does the answer make sense?

Yes.

Use an equation to check your work.

$8 - 8 = 0$

Using Place-Value Drawings

When the numbers in the problem have more than one digit, it can help you to make a place-value drawing.

 Here's the problem.

Under a bridge, 124 small brown bats sleep during the day. Another 132 bats sleep in a nearby barn. Combined, how many bats sleep under the bridge and in the barn?

Bats often live together in large colonies. They sleep during the day and come out to eat at night.

Read and understand.

What do you know?

There are 124 bats sleeping under the bridge.
There are 132 bats sleeping in the barn.

What are you trying to find?

The number of bats in all.

This problem uses three-digit numbers.

Let's use a place-value drawing.

A place-value drawing uses dots for digits in the ones place.

Ten dots joined together form a line for a digit in the tens place.

Ten lines joined together form a box for a digit in the hundreds place.

 Solve.

Using a place-value drawing, draw 124 for the bats under the bridge.

Now draw 132 for the bats in the barn.

Use the place-value drawing to count how many bats in all.

Count the total in each place.

Begin in the ones place.

There are 6 ones.   6

There are 5 tens.   56

There are 2 hundreds.   256

There are 256 bats in all.

 Look back.

Did you start with the right numbers?

Yes.

Using Place-Value Drawing to Add by Regrouping

Sometimes when you add numbers, the total in one place will group into the next larger place.

? Here's the problem.

There were 28 blue dragonflies sitting on a pond. There were 7 green dragonflies on the same pond. In all, how many dragonflies were on the pond?

Dragonflies often live near water. They are hunters and spend their time looking for bugs to eat.

Read and understand.

What do you know?
There were 28 blue dragonflies.
There were 7 green dragonflies.

What are you trying to find?

The number of dragonflies in all.

 ## Plan.

Let's use a place-value drawing.

 ## Solve.

There were 28 blue dragonflies.
Draw 28 using a place-value drawing.
Now draw the 7 more dragonflies that landed.
Ten dots can be grouped into a line.
Circle 10 ones dots.
Cross out the circle, and draw a ten-line.
Use the place-value drawing to count
how many dragonflies in all.
There are 3 tens. There are 5 ones.

28 + 7 = 35

In all, there were 35 dragonflies on the pond.

 ## Look back.

Does the answer match the question? Did you use the right numbers?
Yes.

Using Place-Value Drawings to Subtract by Regrouping

Sometimes when you subtract, you need to break a group from one place value into smaller units.

Here's the problem.

Twenty armadillos were resting in the sun. A coyote scared them, and five of them rolled up into balls. How many did not roll up into a ball?

This is a nine–banded armadillo.

Read and understand.

What do you know?

There were 20 armadillos.

Five rolled up into balls.

What are you trying to find?

How many armadillos did not roll up into a ball.

 ## Plan.

Let's use a place-value drawing.

 ## Solve.

There are 20 armadillos.

Draw 20 using a place-value drawing.

Five of them rolled into balls. Five is in the ones place, but there are no ones in 20.

One ten is the same as ten ones.

Replace one ten with ten ones.

Cross off five ones for the five armadillos that rolled into balls. Count how many are left.

There are fifteen.

$$20 - 5 = 15$$

Fifteen armadillos did not roll up into a ball.

 ## Look back.

Does the answer make sense?

Yes.

Solving Problems with Mental Math

! Using Mental Addition

When numbers end in zeros, you can add or subtract them in your head.

? Here's the problem.

Each hedgehog has about 7,000 quills, or hollow hairs. About how many quills do two hedgehogs have together?

Hedgehogs' quills are not venomous.

Read and understand.

What do you know?

One hedgehog has about 7,000 quills.

What are you trying to find?

The number of quills on two hedgehogs together.

Plan.

Let's use mental math to add the number of quills.

Solve.

7,000 + 7,000

Think:

There are no ones, tens, or hundreds. I only need to add the digits in the thousands place.

7 + 7 = 14, so 7,000 + 7,000 = 14,000

Two hedgehogs together have about 14,000 quills.

Look back.

Did you remember to include the units in your answer?
Yes.

Is your math correct?
Yes, 7,000 + 7,000 = 14,000.

Subtracting in Your Head

You can subtract mentally by using place value.

Here's the problem.

There were 200 electric eels living in the Amazon River basin. A science team carefully collected 112 of the eels to study. How many eels were **left** in the basin?

An electric eel is actually not an eel. It's a knifefish!

Read and understand.

What do you know?

There were 200 eels on the reef.

A team took 112 of the eels.

What are you trying to find?

The number of eels left on the reef.

Are there any clue words?

Yes, the clue word "**left**" tells you to use subtraction.

Plan.

Let's use mental math to subtract.

Solve.

$200 - 112$

You can subtract in your head by thinking of 112 as 100 + 10 + 2, and subtracting in steps.

Start with 200 and subtract the hundreds, 100.

$200 - 100 = 100$

From what is left, 100, subtract the tens, 10.

$100 - 10 = 90$

From what is left (90), subtract the ones (2).

$90 - 2 = 88$

$200 - 112 = 88$

There were 88 electric eels left in the basin.

Look back.

Did you remember to include the units in your answer?

Yes.

Multi-Digit Problems

! Multi-Digit Addition

You can use equations to help you add numbers with more than one digit.

? Here's the problem.

The elephant seal and the sea lion are both kinds of pinnipeds, or fin-footed mammals. There are 128 elephant seals on a beach. There are 263 sea lions on the beach. How many pinnipeds are on the beach?

You can tell this is a sea lion because it has ear flaps you can see. A seal just has small holes on its head.

 ## Read and understand.

What do you know?
There are 128 elephant seals.
There are 263 sea lions.

What are you trying to find?

The number of seals.

What kind of problem is this?

To find the number of seals, you must combine the elephant seals and sea lions. It is an addition problem.

Plan.

Write an addition equation.

Solve.

128 elephant seals + 263 seal lions = total pinnipeds
Numbers with more than one digit are easier to add when you write them in columns to line up the place values.

For the problem:

```
  1
 128
+ 263
_____
```

	Add the tens place. (Don't forget to carry the 1)	
Add the ones place.		Add the hundreds place.
$8 + 3 = 11$	$1 + 2 + 6 = 9$	$1 + 2 = 3$

There are 391 pinnipeds on the beach.

Look back.

Did you answer the right question?

Yes.

Multi-Digit Subtraction

You can write subtraction equations to help you subtract numbers with more than one digit.

Here's the problem.

An aquarium has 140 jellyfish and 34 squid. How many more jellyfish are there than squid?

Read and understand.

What do you know?

There are 140 jellyfish and 34 squid.

What are you trying to find?

The difference between the number of jellyfish and the number of squid.

Are there any clue words?

Yes, "**how many more**" tell you this is a subtraction problem.

The long tendrils on this jellyfish will sting anything that touches them.

Plan.

Write a subtraction equation.

Solve.

Write the numbers in columns to line up the place values.

$$
\begin{array}{r}
140 \\
-\ 34 \\
\hline
\end{array}
$$

Subtract the ones first. Wait a minute! You cannot subtract 4 from 0. What do you do? Borrow 1 ten and group it as 10 ones. You subtract 4 from 10.

Now subtract the tens. Remember you borrowed one so you are subtracting 30 from 30 or 3−3.

There are no hundreds to subtract, so bring down the 1. There are 106 more jellyfish than squid.

$$
\begin{array}{r}
{\scriptstyle 3\ 1} \\
1\!\!\!\!/40 \\
-\ \ 34 \\
\hline
106 \\
\end{array}
$$

Look back.

Does the answer make sense?
Yes.

Is the math correct?
Check your subtraction by adding. 106 + 34 = 140.

It's OK to Estimate

You can use estimation when you do not need to know the exact answer to a problem.

 Here's the problem.

A bison rancher has 189 bison in a corral. He has 214 bison in a large pasture and 176 more in a small pasture. About how many bison does the rancher have in total?

Bison, also called American Buffalo, used to roam the American west in large numbers. Too much hunting almost made them extinct.

Read and understand.

What do you know?

There are 189 bison in the corral.
There are 214 bison in the large pasture.
There are 176 bison in the small pasture.

Is there anything special about this problem?

Yes. The problem asks "about how many."
The "about" tells you the answer does not need to be exact.

What are you trying to find?

An estimate of the total number of bison.

Plan.

Let's estimate the answer by rounding each number to the greatest place value, the hundreds place.

Solve.

Round each number to the hundreds place.

189 rounds to 200
214 rounds to 200
176 rounds to 200

Add the rounded numbers.

$$
\begin{array}{r}
200 \\
200 \\
+\ 200 \\
\hline
600
\end{array}
$$

The rancher has about 600 bison.

Look back.

Does the answer make sense?

Yes.

Did you answer the right question?

Yes.

Remember the Plan!

Now you have new tools to help you solve word problems. Just remember your four-step plan to read and understand, make a plan, solve, and look back. You are ready to tackle more word problems!

Glossary

addition The process of adding two or more numbers together.

equation A number sentence such as 1 + 1= 2, where the expressions on either side of the equals sign are the same.

estimate Take a good guess.

inverse The opposite of something else. In math, addition and subtraction are inverses.

operation A math process, such as addition, subtraction, multiplication, or division.

place value The value of a digit that is based on its position in the number.

regroup Making groups of tens to help make solving math problems easier.

rounding Using a number that is less exact to help solve problems. For example, 13 would round to 10 and 17 would round to 20.

subtraction The process of taking a number away from a larger number.

unit The object that is being added or subtracted, such as spines or stripes.

For More Information

Books

Adler, David A. *You Can, Toucan, Math: Word Problem–Solving Fun.* New York, NY: Holiday House, 2006.

Murphy, Stuart J. *Coyotes All Around.* New York, NY: HarperTrophy, 2003.

Scieszka, Jon. *Math Curse.* New York, NY: Viking, 2007.

Websites

Aplusmath
www.aplusmath.com
Interactive math resources for teachers, parents, and students featuring free math worksheets, math games, math flashcards, and more.

Coolmath Games
www.coolmath-games.com
Try your hand at games that make learning and practicing math fun.

Math Playground
www.mathplayground.com/ wordproblems.html
Solve math word problems with Thinking Blocks, Jake and Astro, and more.

Index

C

clue words
    addition, 8, 13–14, 26, 44
    subtraction, 16, 38, 42
columns, 41, 43

D

draw a picture, 24–25

E

equations
    addition, 10–12, 15
    subtraction, 17, 21, 29, 43
estimation, 44–45
example problems, 7, 10, 15, 18, 20, 21, 24, 26, 28, 30, 32, 34, 36, 38, 40, 42, 44

I

identifying problem types
    addition, 13–14
    subtraction, 15–17, 25
information
    too little, 20–21
    too much, 21–23
inverse operations, 18–19

M

make a chart, 22–23
mental math
    addition, 36–37
    subtraction, 38–39
multi-digit problems
    addition, 40–41
    subtraction, 42–43

O

operations, 13
opposites, 18

P

place-value drawings, 30–35
problem-solving steps, 8–9

R

regrouping,
    addition, 32–33
    subtraction, 34–35
rounding, 44–45

U

units, 9, 27, 34, 37, 39

Z

zeros, 26–29, 36–37